Grolier Enterprises Inc. offers a varied selection of both
adult and children's book racks. For details on ordering
please write: Grolier Enterprises Inc., Sherman Turnpike,
Danbury, CT 06810 Attn: Premium Department

NOW YOU CAN READ. . . .

JOSEPH, MAN OF DREAMS

STORY RETOLD BY ARLENE C. ROURKE

ILLUSTRATED BY GWEN GREEN

Library of Congress Cataloging in Publication Data

Rourke, Arlene, 1944-
  Joseph, man of dreams.

  Summary: A retelling of the Old Testament story of
Joseph whose brothers sold him into slavery in Egypt
and who grew up to become the Pharaoh's trusted
adviser.
  [1. Joseph (Son of Jacob)—Juvenile literature.
2. Bible. O.T.—Biography—Juvenile literature.
[1. Joseph (Son of Jacob) 2. Bible stories—O.T.]
I. Title.
BS580.J6R68 1985   222'.110924 [B]   85-19677
ISBN 0-86625-318-1

GROLIER ENTERPRISES CORP.

NOW YOU CAN READ....
JOSEPH, MAN OF DREAMS

Joseph was a boy who lived in a land called Canaan. His father was named Jacob. Even though Jacob had eleven other sons, he loved Joseph best. One day, he gave Joseph a beautiful coat with many colors.

Joseph's brothers were jealous of him. They were angry that Jacob loved him more than them. Jacob had never given any of them a beautiful coat.

One day, Joseph and his brothers were in the desert. They saw a caravan of merchants coming. Joseph's brothers talked together.

"We will sell Joseph to the merchants and take his coat away from him," said one of them. That is what they did.

After the merchants had taken Joseph, his brothers dipped his beautiful coat in the blood of an animal. They went home and told Jacob that Joseph had been killed by a wild beast.

Now the brothers would never have to see Joseph again!

The merchants brought Joseph to
the land of Egypt. There, they sold
him as a slave. A slave is a person
who must work without pay for his
master. He cannot leave because he
is owned by his master.

Joseph was bought by a man named Potiphar. Potiphar was a rich and important man. He was a general in the army of the king of Egypt. Joseph worked as a servant in Potiphar's big house.

Joseph was a bright young man and did his work well. Everyone liked him. Everyone except Potiphar's wife. She did not like Joseph. She told lies about him and he was sent to prison.

Joseph might have stayed in prison until he died. But, Joseph had a wonderful talent! He could tell people what their dreams meant.

In those days, people believed that you could tell what would happen in the future if you could understand dreams.

The other prisoners would come to Joseph and tell him their dreams. He would tell them what their dreams meant. He was always right. He became famous for explaining people's dreams. Even the Pharoah, the great king of Egypt, had heard of Joseph.

One night, the Pharoah had a dream. The next day he sent for his wise men. He told them his dream and asked them what it meant. None of them could explain it. The Pharoah grew angry. "What good are you to me if you cannot do this simple thing?" he shouted. "I will send for that young man in prison. If he can tell me what my dream means, I will set him free."

And so, Joseph was brought before the Pharoah.

"I was standing near the River Nile," the Pharoah said. "I saw seven fat cows eating grass by the river bank. Along came seven thin cows. They ate the seven fat cows, but did not get fat themselves. What does this mean, Joseph?"

Joseph thought for a moment. Then, he spoke.

"The seven fat cows mean that Egypt will have good harvests for seven years. The seven thin cows mean that seven bad harvests will follow the good ones. Your people will starve unless you save food for the seven bad years."

The Pharoah looked at Joseph. After a while he spoke.

"I believe that what you have said is true. You are a free man, Joseph. Since you are also a wise man, you will be in charge of the food in my land. You will store enough food in the good years to prepare for the seven bad years."

Joseph became a very important man in Egypt. Everything that he told the Pharoah came true. In the good years, there was more food than the people could eat. He stored the extra food.

Then, the bad years came. There was no food. People were starving. Joseph began to give out the food he had stored. There was enough to feed the Egyptian people. Even men from other lands came to get food.

One day, some men came from Canaan. They bowed before Joseph. They were Joseph's brothers.

"Our family is starving. Please let us buy food," said Reuben, the oldest. Reuben and his brothers did not recognize Joseph. It had been many years since they had sold him to the merchants in the desert.

Joseph recognized them. "Don't you know me? I'm your brother, Joseph," he said. His brothers begged his forgiveness.

They felt ashamed for what they had done to him. Joseph hugged them all and forgave them. He knew that God wants us to love and forgive those who do wrong to us.

All these appear in the pages of the story. Can you find them?

Joseph

Potiphar's wife

Jacob

Pharoah

Potiphar

Reuben

Now tell the story in your own words.